Make Easy Money Fast Selling Books
Through Amazon Trade-In and BookScouter

A Comprehensive "How-To" Guide

Steve A Johnson

Publisher's Note

This publication is designed to provide accurate and authoritative information in regard to the subject matter covered. It is sold with the understanding that the publisher is not engaged in rendering psychological, financial, legal, or other professional services. If expert assistance or counseling is needed, the services of a competent professional should be sought.

The fact that a website or organization is referred to in this work as a potential source of further information does not mean that the author or the publisher endorses the information the organization or website may provide or recommendations it may make. Further, readers should be aware that the websites listed in this work may have changed or disappeared between when this work was written and when it is read.

ISBN-13: 978-1520659299

Dedication

To all those individuals and their families who struggle to make financial ends meet.

Table of Contents

Introduction

I am a psychotherapist with absolutely no sense of business or making money other than seeing clients, billing insurance, and collecting co-pays. I am also a professor, so I read lots of books and most never leave my home or office. However, my wife and I are getting ready to clean out the house so we can declutter and downsize our lives. I really need to get rid of many of the books I haven't read in a while, but I just don't like the idea of tossing the ones the public or university libraries didn't want, so I wondered whether I could sell some without the hassle of a yard sale or gate sale. So the search began.

Oh, and I didn't want to have to learn some complicated process that would yield barely enough to buy a large three topping pizza and eat up precious time I could have been using to do something fun like having a meal with my "Fat Guys for Lunch Bunch."

Since I buy a lot of books from Amazon, I thought about creating a business and selling the books through them, but I am essentially lazy and didn't want to have to go through the hassle of right pricing the books, watch what others were charging, making adjustments, calculating profit margin—you get the picture. If you are into that stuff and you have the time, knock yourself out, but it just isn't my thing.

Then I discovered Amazon's Trade-In program, which doesn't yield cash, but does give credit for future purchases. I decided to give it a try, so I went through a brief process I will describe in this book, and the result is that I made enough off my first try to purchase Christmas gifts for my wife and two grown daughters and a few things for myself. I have also been purchasing items for free on Amazon for five months, including Valentine Day gifts for my family plus my mother.

[Although not directly relevant to this book, I have linked one of my credit cards to my Amazon account and have been able to use my credit card points to make additional purchases for free—but I digress.]

I love Amazon's Trade-In program, but encountered a minor hassle, and that was Amazon wasn't interested in purchasing a number of my books, even books I had purchased through them. Therefore, I thought about casting my net wider and to see whether I could find an easy way to find online companies that might be interested in purchasing the books. That is when I discovered BookScouter.com, a fantastic website that did exactly what I was looking for. Well, that isn't entirely true. It exceeded my expectations because it put me in contact with a long list of companies who were looking for the books I wanted to sell AND it told me what they were willing to pay, linked me to their websites so I knew how to box the books for them, and send them off.

I bit the bullet and mailed off my first three boxes in one day. I had virtually no learning curve, so it may have taken me 2 hours to go through the process and schlepp the boxes to Staples where I mailed them for free. In a week I got checks in the amount of $479.23. That is roughly equivalent to three sessions with a client and without having to take notes, complete insurance forms, collect the co-pays, not to mention the cost of the office, insurance, and driving to and from the office.

I was hooked! My wife was happy that I was cleaning the books out of the house, and during this time I had surgery and was unable to work, so it gave me something to do that made a little income and kept me busy.

What I will be doing in this book is walking you through, step-by-step what to do for the Amazon Trade-In program as well as BookScouter. I will share where I purchased everything I needed from quickly cleaning books to packing materials to printing labels for boxes. Keep in mind that the prices I list for some items will change over time and some products may be discontinued, so you may need to look at equivalent products. I recommend that you keep your eye open for discounted products. For example, I first started purchasing boxes at Home Depot, but for small boxes, I found find what I thought was a better deal for me at Ocean State Job Lot

Amazon Trade In

In this section of the book I want to help you learn the simple steps to take to earn credit toward future Amazon purchases by trading in your used books, either books you bought from Amazon or books you didn't purchase from them.

The detailed information in this section will also be valuable for selling your books for cash through BookScouter However, I will cover the details about using BookScouter in a later section of this book.

This section will cover the following information:

>*How to determine how much Amazon Trade In will credit you for each of your books,
>*How to identify free shipping
>*How to print packing slips and package labels for mailing
>*Where to purchase inexpensive packing materials, such as
>>+Heavy duty boxes
>>+Packing tape
>>+Packing paper and bubble wrap
>*How to pack the books/DVD's
>*How to tape a box to avoid problems
>*Where to find books to trade in

General Overview of the Amazon Trade In Program

Amazon says their Trade-In program permits customers to receive an Amazon Gift Card for hundreds of thousands of eligible items. I traded in books and DVDs, but the program permits exchanging phones, electronics, videogames, books, DVDs, and CDs. They go on to say that the entire process is easy and made even easier and more convenient and unviting in that it offers free shipping and an immediate offer is made online. That was my experience with the program. I made a few mistakes with my first box of books, but after that I didn't make any other mistakes and it all went very smoothly.

Amazon also says that depending on where you live, the trade ins can take up to 10 days to arrive at an Amazon center where your submission is processed. My first experience was as a person living in Connecticut, I had one box directed to Kentucky and another to Pennsylvania. The whole process took 2-3 days.

Once the items are received by Amazon and checked, you get an email notification within 2 days. In that email you learn whether the items were accepted or rejected. Again, my experience was that some of my items were accepted, very few rejected, and some items were busy being processed. It seemed to take a little longer to make a decision about DVDs.

Once the accepted trade-in is credited to your Trade-In Account, you can check the amount registered to your gift card. I couldn't believe how fast the process was. My daughter told me she needed a used book about sign language for a course she was taking for fun. It was a pricey book, but only 2 days after I mailed my box, my gift card was credited and I purchased her $102.00 book paid for completely by the gift card and I had several hundred dollars left on the card.

If there was a weak spot in the overall processing, it was Amazon's description of what conditions the book or DVD had to be in to be acceptable. However, in reality it was no problem because I sent only items in very good shape so I had no item rejected for not being in acceptable condition. My experience was that if you send good stuff, there is no problem and you will get the full offering price. Amazon was fair and not into being nitpicky such that would have made me feel they were "nickel and dime-ing" me to death.

The part I very much appreciated was the free shipping and how easy it was to implement. If you use the pre-paid label generated by the computer, the process was easy and totally free. Just print a pre-paid U.S. Postal Service shipping label and drop the box off anywhere that accepts them. You can get right on the Amazon site the exact locations near you with an indicator of the mileage from where you live. It couldn't be easier. Later in this book, I will show you a pre-paid label I used and which was generated from the Amazon site.

If you lose your label before putting it on the box, you can just go to your Trade-In Account and print another label. To avoid this process, I just printed 2 labels in the first place.

If you have more than one box, you must generate a different label for each box after have listed the items in each box. You can't print 2 copies of the same label for the two boxes. Each box gets its own label.

What if you have an item that isn't listed in the Trade-In Store? Can you sell it? No, but there are a couple of ways you can go. One, you can wait and check back with the store in the future and the items may have become needed and thus, you can redeem it. Two, and this is what I did because my wife had ordered (oh so nicely, but firmly) that she didn't want my books piled around the house, so I traded many of the books not accepted by Amazon to other large bookstores that will buy them online. Later in this book I will explain how easy it is to locate through one website the bookstores that are interested in your book along with the price each will pay for the book. You can go with the best price. The entire process is very easy.

Locating Books

I have already mentioned that I had a lot of books around the house. I also had a lot of books in my office, but what do you do once these books have been traded in at Amazon? Well, I looked in several places, such as...

> *Yard sales/garage sales/tag sales
> *Library and church/synagogue book give-aways
> *Flyers in university dorms or bulletin boards outside university departments at the end of a term. Alternatively, you can ask the university officials for permission to put ads up in dorms, around the campus, or in university newspapers. A short ad in the university newspaper toward the end of the term is a good idea depending on the cost of the ad.
> *I had great luck offering some of the books I couldn't trade in to Amazon to churches in exchange for books they wanted to give away.
> *University libraries often have a book give-away once a year, so it is worthwhile to check on those dates
> *Check on estate sales and auctions that may sell books in bulk for a low price.
> *Goodwill and other such stores often have books very cheap.
> [*Later in the book, in the section on using BookScouter, I will discuss how to determine the price for which you could sell these books to online book sellers.*]

For all these abovementioned ways to get books, you can use the Amazon app to determine how much the book is worth in the Amazon Trade-In Store and how much profit you would make after you deduct the price for which you would pay for it. This could help prevent you losing money on the book. *[Later in this section of the book, I will cover the cost of materials for packing and shipping the books so you can get an ever better sense of your profit margin.]* Because I don't buy or sell high volumes, I don't bother getting a book if I am only going to get anything less than $1.00. That said, when it comes to DVDs, I might go under #1.00 because they take so little space ina box, require very little prep (don't require cleaning as a book might), and I don't lose much money due to the price of the box and packing materials, especially when they are included with books for which I will get a decent price.

Your Trade-In Account

Here you will see listed "All Trade-In Orders," "Pending Trade-In Orders," or "Closed Trade-In Orders." For each book you will see your Trade-In Order Number, the date the trade-in order was placed along with some options you can check.

    *Cancel order
    *Re-print shipping label
    *Track your shipment

Also on this page you will find "Your Offer," which is the maximum Amazon will pay for your book. You may receive less contingent on the condition of your book, e.g., the cover is dirty, creased, or the interior contains markings.

Once the box has been received at its Amazon destination and its contents appraised, you will find the "Appraised Value" of the book in your Trade-In Account. That is how much will be credited to your Amazon Gift Card. You will also see the note "Paid." Simply check your Amazon Gift Card Account for the amount in it.

Trading In the Books

Amazon Textbooks Trade In

Go to the following website: https://www.amazon.com/Sell-Books/b?node=2205237011 to begin trading in your books. At that site you will see a section in which you can enter a title, author, or ISBN number. Enter in any of those three items and you will get a heading that includes the following:

*Books
*Trade-In Store
*Submit Your Trade-Ins
*Your Trade-In Account

Below that heading you will see a subheading that reads, "Textbooks Trade-in: Get up to 80% Back."

Still below the subheading will be a clear section in which to enter the book title, author, or ISBN. Once you enter one of those bits of information, you will be directed to a page that lists your buying options for the book. For example, I entered DBT®Skills Training Handouts & Worksheets, Second Edition. I was taken to a page where at the top I saw an icon for the book and information that the spiral bound edition available through Amazon sold for $28.39. There were other options, including new and used books. The Kindle version was available for $22.50.

If you go back to the subheading, you will see, "Trade-In Items You Bought for a Amazon Gift Card. There it will tell you the total value for your previous purchases through Amazon, including books, CDs, DVDs, etc. For example, I saw that I had purchased a book entitled, The MMPI-2/MMPI-2RF and that I could get up to $81.41 if I traded it in to Amazon.

If you scroll down this page, you can see several sections. One you might find helpful is "Best Sellers" and below that you will see a list of books and their trade-in values. I find this section of limited value. For example, today as I was writing this book, there are listed 274,888 such books. That list is simply too long to be of much help to me unless I were to note the top listed items and in my travels come upon them.

If you go back to the page where the heading includes "Trade-In Store," you will see at the top the total amount you could make if you traded in the Amazon items you had previously purchased. Today, I could make $610.57. Below that you can see book icons and a note designating the top trade-in value or a note saying "No trade-in offer available." If you see the latter note, check back later because a book that isn't wanted or needed now, may show up as needed/wanted later. For example, in this section I learned that I could get up to $29.82 if I traded in my book, <u>Relational Concepts in Psychoanalysis</u>, but currently nothing for <u>Clinician's Guide to Mind Over Mood</u>.

Now go back to the heading where you see, "Submit Your Trade-Ins." There you will find your address and shipping method. You can change your address or method of shipping. If you check "change" by the shipping method, you will get a screen where you can choose two ways to ship:

> *UPS Free shipping at any UPS store or drop off location (Estimated delivery time is 2-6 business days). You can click "UPS store or drop off location for the location closest to your address.
> *Carrier of your choice. However, if you choose this option, you will have to pay for the shipping.

You will also find your trade-in list, which if you have mailed the books that you had boxed, you will see a note "You have no items to trade-in."

Below that is an section in which you can enter the name of a book. It doesn't matter, whether you purchased it from Amazon or not. You can search for its maximum trade-in value, if it is worth anything at that time. I typed in the title of a book in my study, <u>An Introduction to Non-Classical Logic</u>, and when I hit "enter" was directed to a place where I saw an icon of the book cover and a note that I could get up to $8.73 if I traded it in.

Below the icon of the book cover, I checked, "Trade in" and was directed to a section in which I could select the condition of the book. For this book I had to answer "yes" or "no" to the following questions:

*Is the cover binding intact?
*Are the pages torn or have major wrinkling from water?
*Are there notes or names on the cover?
*Do the pages have excessive writing or highlighting?

If you check that one of the negative conditions is true for this book, then you will get a note that unfortunately you can't trade it in. If the conditions are satisfactory, then you will be directed to check the ISBN found on the back of the book, usually in the lower right hand corner. You will check whether the ISBN matches the one listed on the website.

You will be asked to verify that the ISBNs match. If they do, then you will be directed back to "Your Trade-In List." At that point you will be asked what you want Amazon to do if they judge the book to be in unsatisfactory condition. Amazon is willing to mail the book back to you for free.

On the same page you will see the "Trade-In Summary" which lists the total you will be credited after Amazon receives the book, along with a note that the shipping is free. You then will be asked to confirm the trade-in.

If you have additional books, you can on this page enter their title and go through the same process you just completed for your book.

If you go back to the original page and clock "Your Trade-in Account," you will get an exhaustive list of books, the status of your offer, the appraised value, how much paid or whether the offer was cancelled or is pending, the trade-in order #, and the date the order was placed.

Once you click "Confirm Trade In" you will be directed to print the label for free shipping. If the label doesn't print well; e.g., the bar code smears, you can go to the "Your Trade In Account" where you have several options:

>   *Cancel order
>   *Re-print shipping label
>   *Track your shipment

Prepping and Packing the Books

<u>Cleaning the Books</u>

Before packing the books, it is important to clean the cover if it is dirty or there are stickers on it. Sometimes someone will have taped a label over the ISBN such that it can be read. When that happens or to clean the book generally, I use "GooGone". I tend to use the spray version of the gel for convenience. I simply spray it on the dirty spot or the label/sticker, wait a few seconds, and then wipe off. Sometimes with the label/sticker I just gently use a razor blade or sharp knife to scrape off the label if it hasn't come off with a pull or two. Be careful that you do not scrape so deeply that you scrape away the ISBN.

Packing the Books

After you have checked whether Amazon will accept your book and what price they will offer you, I recommend you do a trial packing of the books in the box without packing material or without taping the top of the box shut. This will permit you to pack as many books as possible without making the box too heavy (it shouldn't be over 50 pounds).

Of course you should tape the bottom of the box and reinforce the edges of the box with tape before you try this trial packing. By the way, I recommend you tape the bottom seam with tape at least three times and each of the edges of the box, 1-2 times. This will minimize the boxes breaking during transit. When I do the trial packing, I do the following:

> *Place the bigger boxes at the bottom, especially hardback books
> *Place the spine of the books outward rather than toward the center of the box
> *Always lay the books flat
> *Place paperback books on the top of the larger hardback books to protect the paperback books from getting bent or otherwise misshapen
> *Place smaller hardback books over the paperback books toward the top of the box

Don't use the packing material yet. Once the books are in place and look secure; i.e., won't shift around too much during shipping, take the books out and place them on a table or the floor in piles so you can easily put them back in the same order for the final packing.

Once you have completed the trial packing and all the books are out of the box, place several sheets of packing material in each of the four bottom corners and along each edge. I like to twist the sheets before placing them in the box for more cushion.

Place the books in the box in the order you took them out to maintain the order they were in during the trial packing. Be sure to place twisted packing materials up all four sides of the box all the way to the top as you add the books. Be sure to make the box as full as possible without going over 50 pounds (I try never to go over 40 pounds because 50 pounds is just a bit too heavy for me if I have to carry them very far when I get to the shipping location). I like to place some bubble wrap in the middle of the two vertical rows of books to help minimize shifting during transit. [If you order frequently from Amazon, you may have some of the air-filled wrap they use, which is great to use if not too thick for your purposes.]

Once all the books are in the box and the bubble wrap is in place, I like to place a few sheets of packing paper on top, and sometimes I even use pieces of cardboard. Hey, I am neurotic and don't want to books damaged. I have never had a book damaged and I always receive the full offered price if the book is accepted.

Before sealing the top of the box with three pieces of packing tape, remember to place a copy of the packing sheet on top. Then seal the box.

Once the box is sealed, print a fairly large copy of the address label and tape it down on the top of the box off to the side and not over the taped seam in the middle. Remember two important things about the label:

*Print the label using a printer where the ink will not run. This is important for the bar code that will be scanned in transit

I recommend that when you tape the address label to the box, you do not tape over the bar code. It only happened to me once, but the tap somehow made it impossible to scan the bar code. I had to take the box back home and print and tape a new address label, which is easy—but it is a hassle.

Now schlepp the box to the shipping location and wait to receive an email from Amazon that the box has been received and is in the process of being assessed.

Purchasing all Packing Materials

In this section I will describe all the materials I use for packing the books, CDs, and DVDs. Be forewarned that all this information was what I found at stores and online at the time of writing this book and may have changed when you purchase the materials. Also, if you find better deals, go for them. This is just what I found, and I offer this not as a recommendation but simply for informational purposes.

Boxes

I have great success using 16x12x12 Heavy-Duty small boxes purchased from Home Depot. At the time I purchased my last order of boxes, they were $1.57 per box—purchased at the store.

Model # 1001016
Internet # 202897299
Store SKU# 523607

Reviews online about these Home Depot boxes indicate that they have been successfully mailed to U.S. soldiers overseas without them breaking open. I used boxes that weren't heavy duty, only to have them break or rip after I had packed them with books weighing under 39 pounds. Home Depot claims their heavy duty small boxes can hold up to 85 pounds.

Tape

I purchased my packing tape at Home Depot. I started out with one 3M Scotch 1.88x54.6 yards Heavy Duty Shipping Packaging Tape and Dispensers for $5.97.

> Model# 3850-RD-DC
> Internet# 100149185
> Store SKU# 545597

At the time I could get a 3-pack for just $9.98.

> Model 3850-LR3-DC
> Internet# 202258943
> Store SKU# 200056

The same brand was available at the time on Amazon, 6 Rolls with dispenser for $13.99.

Packing Paper

This stuff is essential as much as I hate buying it. You may avoid purchasing much of it if you order a lot of items and they are packed with decent packing paper. I especially like the light weight corrugated packing paper—not as heavy as the corrugated cardboard used to make boxes. This stuff is great for packing books. However, the first time I shipped boxes in Amazon's Trade-In program, I hadn't saved any such material, so I had to purchase packing paper.

I purchased mine at Home Depot, although it was more expensive than I had wanted to pay. It was, however, convenient, since it was located in the store by the boxes and packing tape. At that time I purchased 2 tapes of 24" x 24" packing paper (70 sheets) for $5.97 per roll. Not knowing how much I would use, I could have gotten by with 1 roll for packing approximately 5-6 boxes.

> Model# 4004001

Internet# 202029374
Store SKU# 627021

I found some available on Amazon sold in larger quantities that would have prevented me from running back and forth to Hope Depot.

Cheap Cheap Moving Box Packing Paper
Large Bundle, 24x36, 325 sheets
$26.99 + Free Shipping

Never use newspaper print in place of packing paper. The newspaper print can bleed ink on the books and make a mess, getting your books rejected by Amazon.

Bubble Wrap

I like using bubble wrap between CDs and DVDs rather than packing paper. I find that it protects the items better. I still use packing paper to line the outside of the boxes because it is effective and cheaper than the bubble wrap. Again, I see bubble wrap used to package items I buy, including items I purchase from Amazon.

From Home Depot I purchased 3/16" x 12" x 36' Bubble Cushion for $7.48 each.

Model# 2002002
Internet# 202029368

On Amazon I found some in larger quantities;

West Pack Shop
3/16" x 175' x 12"
Small Bubble Cushioning Wrap
$20.00
Or
3/16" x 350' x 12" (Save 20%)

$18.00—Free Shipping

BookScouter

There are times when Amazon's Trade-In program won't purchase a book or times when I am not happy with how much Amazon will pay for a particular book. Therefore, I like having options and one option that is a very convenient one-stop place to locate online book sellers that may buy the book or pay more than Amazon would is BookScouter.

What do I like about BookScouter (which is located at BookScouter.com)?

*It lists 41 book vendors that will buy books
*You can compare the vendors for the purchase price of any given book—and it lists what Amazon is currently paying
*You can read the particular requirements for each vendor so you know information about...
    *What each vendor will purchase: books, DVDs, CDs, or electronics
    *Whether there is a minimum total combined book value in order to receive free shipping
    *Mode of payment, i.e., check, PayPal, or store credit
    *Whether there is a maximum weight limit per box shipped

Let's use a concrete example of the information given for a single book you may want to sell. I will use a book I mentioned in relation to Amazon's Trade-In program, namely, Relational Concepts in Psychoanalysis: An Integration by Stephen A. Mitchell.

Go to BookScouter.com and where you find "Search and ISBN" simply enter the book's ISBN, which in this case is 0-674-75411-5. When I did so, I discovered that its sales rank on Amazon was 237,624 and there are 64 Amazon sellers beginning at $34.92. At this time Amazon was offering the highest price at $25.54 buy back for credit. If I clicked on that, I would be taken to the Amazon

Trade-In Store where I could submit the book for purchase by following the rules I have gave in section 1 of this book.

However, let's say that you wanted to see several books and Amazon wasn't buying very many of them, or you wanted to know whether another seller was purchasing the other books as well as this particular book, so to avoid selling to different vendors you wanted to send to the one that offered the highest average price for the books.

In this instance there were several vendors willing to purchase the book, including the following:

*TextbookRush for $18,61
*SellBackYourBook for $7.96
*BookStore for $7.46
*Buyback Express for $6.09
*Powell's for $3.25
*Bookbyte for $2.75
*TextbookRecycling for $0.90

As you can see there is great variety in the prices you would receive for the book. Let's say you decide that you want to sell your book back to TextbookRush for $18.61. What do you do?

To the right of the price of $18.61 is a "Sell" button. When I clicked on that button, I saw an icon for the book cover as well as two prices: one for a store credit, which in this case was $19.54, and a purchase price of $18.61. To the right of these amounts was a "Add to Sell Cart." If you want to see to them, click the button and follow the directions for book submission requirements, including packaging along with shipping instructions.

The process is similar for all the vendors. You will just need to be sure you read the FAQ section for any given vendor so you get the particulars for that vendor. You also want to make sure you designate your preferred method of payment and whether the vendor offers payment or a store credit.

When will you get paid? It depends on the vendor. Given the type books I sell, I often use TextbookRush or SellBackYourBook and it usually just takes a few days to a week or two for me to get a check mailed to me. Both have been excellent about sending email messages about the status and progress of the order.

I also like the occasional emails from them indicating times of the year when textbooks are in demand. I have found that August and December/January to be the times when I can get the best prices for my books, especially if I am selling books used in university courses.

Made in the USA
Columbia, SC
27 October 2023

25062954R00017